Keep Moving Forward, Henry!

An Inspiring Story of Perseverance
in the Face of Racism

ISBN 978-1-954781-00-9

Thank you, Dad, for showing me
how to persevere and to keep
moving forward! This book is
dedicated to all the firefighters who
help keep our communities safe!

-A.M.

I want to thank my parents for
supporting me all the time, without
you, my life wouldn't be the same.
And thank you Ayanna for letting
me be a part of this beautiful project.

- Estefania Razo

Keep Moving Forward, Henry!

An Inspiring Story of Perseverance in the Face of Racism

Ayanna Murray

Illustrated by Estefanía Razo

At 3 o'clock in the morning, the fire alarm blared and pushed us out of bed.

I was honored to serve as one of the first African-American firefighters in my city.
Congratulations, Henry.
Thank you, sir.
EUGENE
DUTY HONOR SERVICE
FIRE & EMS

I was trained to run into burning buildings, not out.

My job was to be fearless and rescue people from danger.

WHEE-OOOO!!
WHEE-OOOO!!

The horns and sirens
hollered and yelled,
letting people know
help was on the way.

Everyone on our firetruck had a job. The Captain gave the orders, and the driver was in charge of the water for the hose.

The lieutenant would follow my
lead into the fire and I would be
the first person to enter the building.

Got it,
Captain!

Henry,
let's put this
fire out!

Opening the door,
I was immediately
ambushed by a cloud
of hot air and a
blazing fireball
blasting above my head!

HENRY, LOOK OUT!

As the hoseman,
my job was to slide
into the flames and
blast away!
SPLASH!
SIZZLE!
CRACKLE!

Pretty soon the
other big fire trucks
arrived to give us
support.

SPLASH!
CHOP!
Break that window!
CRASH!

Firemen are trained to endure these dangerous conditions.
As the hoseman it was my job to be the first to go in and last to get out.

EUGENE
FIRE & EMS
DUTY HONOR SERVICE

Back at the firestation I wanted to recover and relax, but the other firemen made this difficult for me. As one of the first African American firemen, I also had to fight flames of hate.
No Henry, YOU have to stay in your uniform.

I've never worked with a black man before.
He's not one of us!

Many of the men did not think I should be allowed to serve as a fireman. Like bullies they were hoping that if they were mean enough, that I would give up and quit.

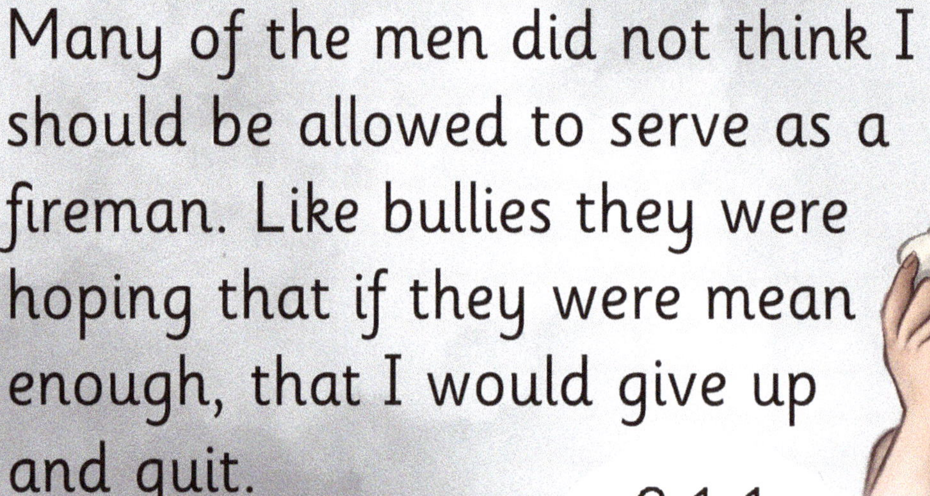

Station 11, we have an emergency.
We're not taking orders from you!
If you don't, that man will die!

It was hard living with men who made it clear they didn't want me around, but I was willing to endure the terrible working conditions just like the men, women, and children who marched for my freedom.

But my dream to serve as a fireman ended abruptly.

The entire department was laid off due to shortage of funds.

Every day I waited to serve again and eventually they called everyone back to work.

Everyone except me.

I felt discouraged.

They actually stopped me
from fighting fires.

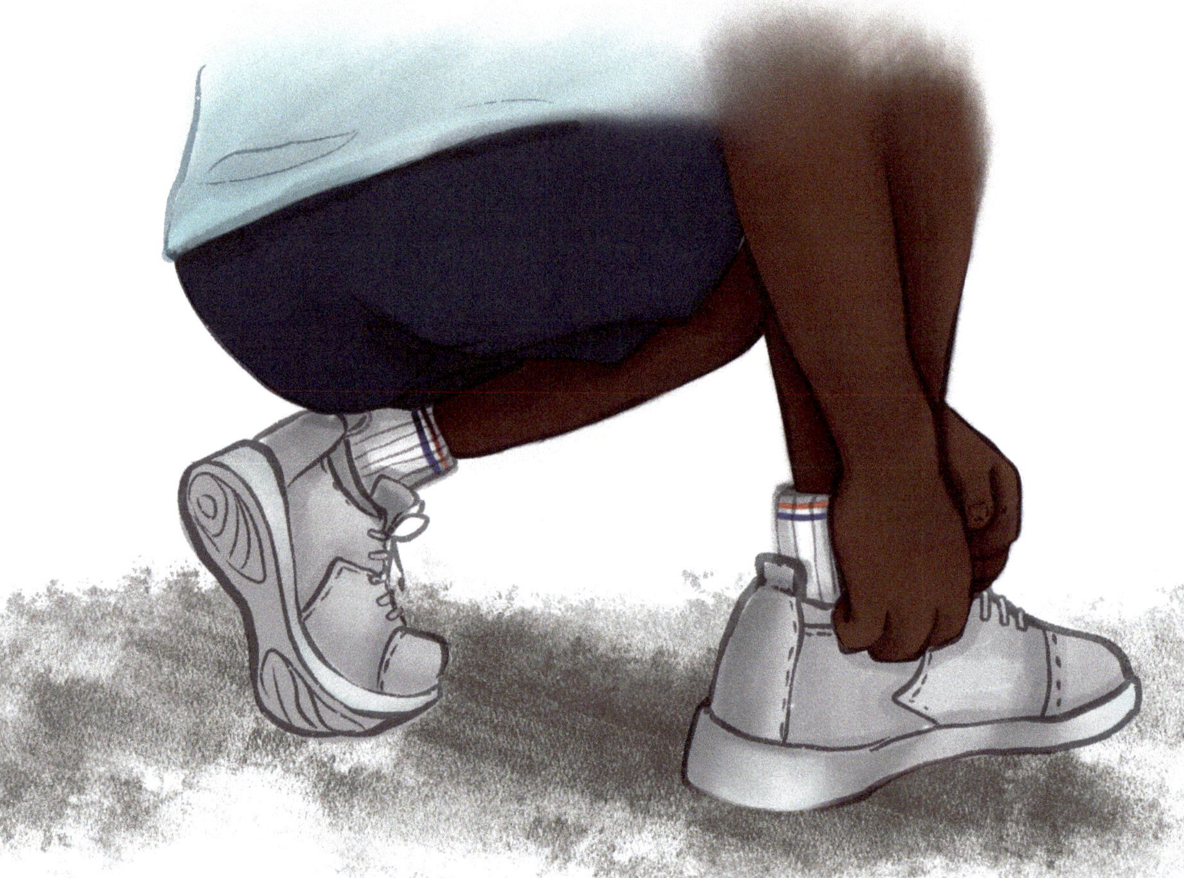

It was then that I felt the strength
and courage of my ancestors rushing
through my veins and saying,

"You'll get knocked down but don't give up.
Keep moving forward, Henry!"

Once I reached the top of the hill, I looked at my hands. My hands were special. They could hold more than a hose. They could hold more than one dream.

AUTHOR'S NOTE

After the 1960's Civil Rights Movement more African American families tried to integrate into all parts of American society. Before the Civil Rights Movement, signs like "Whites Only" appeared in windows, preventing black people from entering or being hired for certain jobs. By the early 1970's many laws had changed but there were still some hearts that were not accepting of Black Americans.

"Keep Moving Forward, Henry" is based loosely on my father's life experience as a fireman and dispatcher. In 1976, my father Henry Luvert and my mother moved from Chicago, IL. and ventured to lay down roots in a predominately white town called Eugene, Oregon. It was in Eugene that my father became one of the first African American firemen and dispatchers in the city.

Henry encountered a barrage of racist and hateful events at the fire station but this never stopped him from going to work and pursuing his dreams. After less than a year of being on the job, his entire graduating class of firemen were laid off. However, within a year, everyone except my father was called back to work. This act of discrimination albeit hurtful did not stop him from moving on with his life and career. He opened up a computer store called "Computer and Software Brokers," later renamed "Graphic Innovators." It was one of the first black computer-operated businesses to the west of the Mississippi. The store ran successfully in downtown Eugene for over ten years. Decades later, the fire lieutenant apologized to my father for how they treated him.

NATIONAL AND OREGONIAN CIVIL RIGHTS TIMELINE 1950-1990

1950—Many rural and small towns outside of Portland, Oregon, had "sundown" laws that were not written into the official books but enforced by police and citizens. The law meant black people needed to be out of town by nightfall or face dangerous and harmful physical consequences.

1953—Oregon's Civil Rights Bill was signed by Governor Paul L. Patterson, making Oregon the twenty-first state in the union to pass legislation outlawing discrimination in public places.

1954—The Supreme Court rules segregation in public schools unconstitutional in the case of Brown v. Board of Education of Topeka, Kansas. As a result black and white children were allowed to attend school together.

1955—Rosa Parks refused to give up her seat on a city bus in Montgomery, Alabama, which led to the Montgomery Bus Boycott.

1957—The Oregon Fair Housing Act passed making the practice of discrimination against African Americans in buying and renting places to live illegal.

1960—The North Carolina Greensboro Sit-Ins occured and Ruby Bridges integrated Frantz Elementary School in New Orleans.

1961—Freedom Rides took place to protest against segregated bus terminals.

1962—The NAACP charged Portland, Oregon, with having racially segregated schools.

1963—Dr. King delivered his "I have a Dream Speech" at the March on Washington.

1964—The Civil Rights Act of 1964 outlawed racial segregation in schools and public places.

1965—President Johnson signed the Voting Rights Act of 1965 to prevent the use of literacy tests as a voting requirement. The busing of African American students began in Portland, Oregon, to desegregate schools.

1967—The Supreme Court ruled that interacial marriages would be legal in the United States.

1968—Dr. Martin Luther King Jr. was assassinated in Memphis, Tennessee, and four days later, President Johnson signed the Civil Rights Act to provide equal housing for all people.

1970—Voting Rights Act was signed into law on July 18, 1970 by President Richard Van Dyke. The law banned and made it a felony for any person or institution to intentionally deny any eligible citizen to vote through any form of coercion, loophole, or other "unconstitutional test."

1971—In the Griggs v. Duke Power Company it was determined that not only is intentional racial discrimination prohibited, but also the hiring and employment policies that continued the effects of past discrimination.

1972—New York Congresswoman Shirley Chisolm became the first African American woman to campaign for the Democratic presidential nomination.

1974—Bill McCoy became the first African American to serve as an Oregon senator.

1976—Henry Luvert and his family moved from the inner city of Chicago to the state of Oregon.

1979—In the United Steelworkers of America v. Weber case, the Supreme Court ruled that

the private sector could apply voluntary racial preference programs in hiring, but many white conservatives viewed it as reverse discrimination.

1980—Oregon became one of the largest recruiting and destination spots for the white supremacist and neo-nazi skinheads.

1981—Henry Luvert was hired as one of the first African American firefighters and dispatchers for the Eugene, Oregon, fire department. In addition, two policemen admitted to racial harassment when they placed four dead possums in front of the Burger Barn, a popular black-owned business in Portland, Oregon.

1982—Henry Luvert was laid off from the Eugene, Oregon fire department due to funding cuts. All of the other firemen who were laid off with him were rehired, but Henry was never offered the opportunity to return as a fireman.

1985—In Oregon, Lloyd Stevenson, a black man, was killed by a policeman using a choke hold. Neither of the two officers involved were disciplined. On the day of Stevenson's funeral, two police officers sold t-shirts to fellow officers with the slogan "Don't Choke 'Em, Smoke 'Em."

1988—President Reagan cut funding for the Equal Employment Opportunity Commission and the Civil Rights Division of the Justice Department. This ensured that most cases of segregation in schools or housing at the Justice Department went uninvestigated. In Portland, Oregon a 28 year old Ethiopian student and father, Mulugeta Seraw, was beaten to death by three racist skinheads.

1990—White supremacist groups like the skin heads and the White Aryan Resistance were growing and thriving in Oregon.

EDUCATIONAL RESOURCES

To Learn about the Civil Rights Movement in Oregon
https://mnch.uoregon.edu/index.php/learn/oregons-civil-rights-movement

The Oregon Historical Society: Racing to Change Oregons' Civil Rights Years
https://www.ohs.org/museum/exhibits/racing-to-change-oregons-civil-rights-years.cfm

PBS Video on History of Racism in Oregon
https://watch.opb.org/video/opb-specials-local-color/

The Oregon Encyclopedia: Blacks in Oregon
https://www.oregonencyclopedia.org/articles/blacks_in_oregon/

African American Firefighter Museum
www.aaffmuseum.org

WORKS CONSULTED

"Oregon Civil Rights Bill," https://www.oregonhistoryproject.org/articles/historical-records/signing-oregon39s-civil-rights-bill-1953/

"1844-1974: A timeline of Oregon discrimination," https://bit.ly/3a2CLkb

"Affirmative Action," https://u-s-history.com/pages/h1970.html

"The Reagan Era: Turning Back Racial Equality Gains," https://bit.ly/36ZKFsv
 Rector, E. (2010),

Looking Back In Order to Move Forward An Often Untold History Affecting Oregon's Past, Present and Future Timeline of Oregon and U.S. Racial, Immigration and Education History [PDF file] https://www.portlandoregon.gov/civic/article/516558

Ayanna Murray

has a Bachelor of Arts degree in Education from the University of Oregon. Ayanna's first published book was Bear Learns to Share, co-authored and illustrated by her daughters, Anaya and Jayda Murray. A homeschool educator for more than a decade, she was born and raised in Eugene, Oregon, where as a little girl she watched and observed her parents fight to overcome racial discrimination. She now lives in Memphis, Tenessee with her husband and four beautiful children.

You can visit Ayanna Murray at www.ayannamurray.com or follow her on Facebook @BooksByAyannaMurray

Estefanía Razo

has a Bachelor of Graphic Design degree from the University of Guadalajara. Estefanía is passionate about illustration, animation and art in general. During her free time, she enjoys reading children's books with her nephews and watching movies accompanied of her cats.

You can visit Estefanía Razo at www.behance.net/argmis or follow her on Instagram as @agmisrzo and dribbble as @Agmis

ALSO AVAILABLE

Keep Moving Forward, Henry! Coloring & Activity Book
ISBN 978-1-954781-01-6

¡Sigue Avanzando, Henry! (Spanish Version) Paperback
ISBN 978-1-954781-04-7

Keep Moving Forward, Henry! E-Book (English)
ISBN 978-1-954781-02-3

¡Sigue Avanzando, Henry! E-Book (Spanish)
ISBN 978-1-954781-06-1

Learn more about the Author on Facebook@ BooksByAyannaMurray